Retold by Kathryn Smith
Illustrated by Stuart Trotter
Religious consultant: Meryl Doney
Language consultant: Betty Root

This is a Parragon Publishing book
First published in 2004

Parragon Publishing
Queen Street House
4 Queen Street
BATH BA1 1HE, UK

Printed in Indonesia

STORIES FROM THE BIBLE

Noah's Ark

p

When God made the world, it was good and beautiful. But the more He watched His people, the sadder He became. They had become selfish and greedy. They hurt each other and the beautiful world He had given them.

Everywhere God looked, He saw anger and cruelty, hatred and fighting. There was only one good man left, who loved and trusted God. His name was Noah.

"I will wash away the wickedness with a flood," God decided. "The world must have a new start."

God chose Noah to help Him.
"I want to make the world
beautiful again," He told Noah.
"Will you help me?"
"Of course," replied Noah,
amazed that God had chosen him.
"What must I do?"

"I will send a great big flood to wash the world clean," said God. "But I will save your family and two of every living creature. You must build an enormous boat and call it an ark. Make it big enough to shelter everyone from the flood."

Noah and his family had never seen a flood before. But they trusted God, so they got to work building the ark, just the way God said.

CHIPPETY CHOP!

BANG!
WHACK!
BANG!

Everyone soon heard about the ark. People came from all around to see it, and to laugh at Noah and his family.

"That boat won't float!" they jeered. "There's no water!"

They wouldn't listen when Noah told them about God's plans.

When the ark was ready, Noah and his family filled it with enough food for everyone. Then they waited.

RUMBLE! RUMBLE!

A huge cloud of dust appeared in the distance.

RUMBLE! RUMBLE! RUMBLE!

The dust cloud got bigger and bigger,
and the noise got louder and louder.

"Watch out!" cried Mrs. Noah.
"God has sent the animals!"

God sent ...

animals that scurry,
animals that creep,
animals that slither,
animals that sneak ...

animals that grunt,
animals that quack,
animals that carry
babies on their back ...

animals that bark,
animals that roar,
animals that snuffle,
and many, many more ...

animals that squawk,
animals that moo,
animals that purr ...

14

and they all came
two-by-two.

Noah carefully counted the animals aboard. When everyone was safely inside, God shut the doors, and it began to rain.

The rain fell softly at first.
DRIP DROP! Then it rained
harder. PITTER PATTER!
Finally, it poured. SPLISH SPLASH!
What a storm! The wind howled,
lightning flashed, thunder crashed.
And the rain just kept on falling.
Streams and rivers burst their banks,
and lakes overflowed, flooding the land.

As the flood water rose, Noah's ark rocked

this way a little, then that way a little.
This way, then that way. This way, that way.

Then it gave an enormous groan, as the
flood waters lifted it.
"Hooray!" cried Noah. "We're afloat!"

For forty days and nights it rained
without stopping. The flood water
rose higher and higher, until even the
tallest trees on the tallest mountains
disappeared. But Noah, his family, and
the animals were safe and warm inside.

Of course, it wasn't easy living on a floating zoo.
It was very dark inside, and the noise was terrible.

The animals
had to be fed,

and exercised
every morning.

And someone had to
clean out all the pens.

POOH!

But Noah and his family never got
downhearted. They just kept trusting in God.

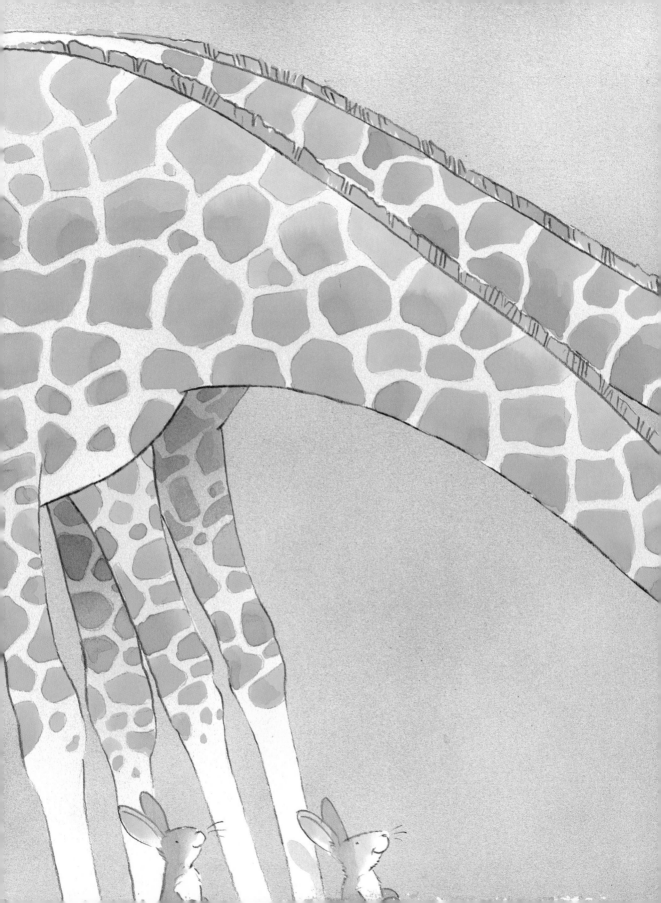

One morning, Noah was busy
doing his rounds, when suddenly
he stopped.

"**LISTEN!**" he cried. His family and
the animals listened, too. Something
had happened, something **VERY**
important. It had stopped raining!

"Now what shall we do?" asked
Noah's sons, looking over the side.

"We must wait," smiled Noah. "God
will not forget us."

For weeks they drifted across the
calm sea, just waiting. Finally the ark
stopped, stuck on the top of a tall
mountain. Slowly, slowly, the flood
water was going down.

One day, Noah set free a raven to look
for land. But the bird couldn't find a
place to rest, and flew back to the ark.
"We must wait just a little longer,"
said Noah.

Noah waited for six long, watery weeks. Then he sent out a dove.

"Bring us a sign," he called as the bird flew off.

All day long Noah and the animals watched and waited.

Just before nightfall, when they had nearly given up hope, they heard the gentle flap of wings.

"She's back!" cried Noah, pointing excitedly. "And look in her beak!" It was a real olive tree twig. "There must be trees poking out of the water!"

Noah waited another week, then sent
out the dove again. And this time, she
didn't come back. She had found dry land.
"It's time to leave the ark!" cried
Noah joyfully. "Thank you, God,
for keeping us safe!"

God was joyful, too.

"This is a new start for the world," He told Noah. "Let your family and the animals out into the sunshine. Go and make new homes, and fill the Earth with new life!"

So Noah threw open the doors.

Out charged the animals, kicking their heels and calling at the tops of their voices.

Then God painted a rainbow in the sky.
"This is a sign of my love," He said. "I will
never wash away the world again. Whenever
the sun shines after the rain, I will put a
rainbow in the sky to remind you of my promise!"